The Essential Book of SHAKER
Discovering the Design, Function, and Form

David Larkin

UNIVERSE PUBLISHING

First published in the United States of America in 1995 by
UNIVERSE PUBLISHING
A Division of Rizzoli International Publications, Inc.
300 Park Avenue South
New York, NY 10010

95 96 97 98 99 / 10 9 8 7 6 5 4 3 2 1

Printed in Singapore

Library of Congress Cataloging-in-Publication Number: 95-060821

GIVEN THE BEAUTY, the efficiency, the grace, and the remarkable craftsmanship of Shaker furniture, buildings, and objects, it is easy to forget that they were the expressions of a religious sect. Shaker designs were not only inspired by a desire for a certain way of life, but were products of actual tenets called the Millenial Laws. Although we may associate certain objects stylistically with the Shakers, we must also realize how intrinsically their aesthetic was linked to their beliefs.

In 1774 thirty-nine-year-old Ann Lee, accompanied by a few followers, arrived in New York from Manchester in England. Based on philosophies that Ann Lee had begun espousing in her homeland, she brought the beginnings of the Shaker movement to America, where she felt they could live and worship more freely. Believing that achieving Utopian harmony on earth was possible if one lived as Christ did, Ann Lee set about establishing an Eden before the fall: a community in which men and women lived together celibately and as equals; where material goods were shunned, and the greed, violence, and insignificant worries of the World (all society outside the Shaker community) were nonexistent. The original and correct name for the group is the United Believers; as the name suggests, union and equality were most important to this sect. The central ideas were those of good-ness, trust, and hard work; the community operated on the idea that individuals should give what they could, and take according to their needs. Making important sacrifices—namely foregoing marriage, private property, and contact with outsiders—would lead to the second coming of Christ within any person.

In reality such ideals were hard won. Mother Ann and her earliest followers were subject to persecution, suffered poverty, and were abondoned by nonbelieving friends and family. Then in the late 1700s a wave of religious fervor hit New York State and New England, in the aftermath of the American Revolution. Attracted to the orderliness and comfort of a self-contained religious sect, the number of converts—who came seeking a peaceful and more structured way of life—grew and Shaker communities were established throughout the region.

In 1784, at the height of this enthusiasm, Mother Ann died. Leadership was taken over by James Whittaker, until his death three years later. Lucy Meacham and Joseph Wright succeeded Whittaker; when Wright died in 1796, Mother Lucy alone headed the Shakers and continued overseeing the flourishing group. In the years since Mother Ann's death, the Shaker influence had spread westward, with new communities established in Kentucky and Ohio.

By 1825 the Shakers numbered 2,500 members. The ideals of communal living—especially without any precedent to follow—were put to the test. At first learning to place the group before the self was difficult. With such an increase in converts, space was cramped and food rations were small.

In addition, the Shakers were the first to attempt communal living while espousing celibacy.

The first Shaker community had been established in New Lebanon, New York, where Mother Lucy resided. Being the central spiritual authority, the "Holy Mount," as it was known, served as the model for all other Shaker societies. Elders and Eldresses from each community were required to visit New Lebanon at least once a year. Given the difficulties in travel, this speaks of the great faith and dedication with which the Shakers lived.

The Shaker communities were organized around Families—or what would be considered a neighborhood in the World. Families were located approximately one-quarter to one-half mile from one another and each had its own workshops, barns, and dwelling spaces. Within every Family existed a hierarchy of Elders and Eldresses, Deacons and Deaconesses, Trustees and Office Sisters. Spiritual guidance, business matters, and household chores were among the responsibilities assigned to these leaders.

In governmental matters, the Shakers were egalitarian—God loves all people—and as such were very progressive in their attitude toward both African-Americans and women. Authority was assigned on the basis of good sense, cooperativeness, and competence. These were the standards for Mother Ann's choices and they remained so. Elders and Elderesses were looked on as parents who lead by example not by decree, quite the opposite of the power structure in the World.

As early as 1800 the daily patterns of Shaker life had been well established and were then consistently adopted by each community. Six days a week were dedicated to labor, with two meal breaks a day, and evenings spent in prayer and socializing. Sunday was a day of rest and worship. Farming was the main source of income in the communities, but weaving, cooking, preserving, furniture and craftsmaking, and seed production brought in supplemental earning through sales to outsiders.

Unity was the goal within the Shaker populace, and they sought that unity in the appearances of their communities as well. The idea that form followed function was behind the way in which the Shakers lived and created; therefore, if theirs was a unified sect, their buildings and wares should reflect this. This was an early idea of Mother Ann's: outward appearance was representative of inner spirituality. Worldly distractions should be shunned as they simply served to drain the spirit. Cleanliness, order, and efficiency were insisted upon; anything that did not serve a purpose should not be added. Mother Ann believed that work should benefit the spirit as well as produce a needed good. Creating something taught patience, which was necessary for true unity.

The earliest Shaker homes were simple frame houses. It is the meetinghouses that are the first true examples of a recognizable Shaker style. Adapted from the gambrel-roofed buildings seen by first-generation converts during their experiences in the World, meetinghouses were the first buildings created solely to fit the Shakers' own needs. White-painted exteriors distinguished meetinghouses from homes and workplaces; the spacious main floors permitted the Shakers to dance in worship. Early United Believer worship was marked by its unusual and uncontrollable "shaking" (from which the name Shaker was derived).

The meetinghouse at Hancock, Massachusetts.

By the time numerous communities had been established, this unorthodox form of worship was translated into actual celebratory dance. The meetinghouse that served as the prototype was originally built at New Lebanon, and master builder Moses Johnson followed this in shape, color, size, and detail throughout New England and New York.

By the 1820s Shaker design had evolved into the classic forms we now recognize as quintessential of the group. The result of westward expansion, increase in membership—and hence, in resources, manpower, and time—and overall optimism, lead to this period of the Shakers' highest achievements. Many new buildings were constructed by believers now less intent on exact duplication of the buildings at New Lebanon. The western communities felt greater freedom to experiment with design, being further removed from the observance of the New Lebanon leaders. Such examples of the amazing craftsmanship of this time include the dual free-standing spiral staircase and the storage units with cupboards and drawers. "Do not make what is not useful" was the credo, and all unnecessary ornamentation was avoided. Objects were created to be long-lasting and allow the greatest efficiency—chairs were built to be easily stored, rooms were designed for easiest clean-up.

Although Worldly contemporaries dismissed Shaker creations as plain and unfashionable, they remain valued today as testimony to the care and craftsmanship of these people. The graceful, beautiful, yet functional designs were the result of their life-style, which was not duplicatible else-where: with no distractions or unimportant daily decisions, the Shakers had a large amount of time, ample resources, and an uncluttered mindframe, which lent itself to such meticulous craftsmanship. From their experience in the World, they were able to adapt Worldly objects and methods, as well as techniques and materials, to their needs. They also had large amounts of time, unrealistic in Worldly societies, designated to crafting not only the articles or buildings themselves but the individual elements needed. For example, Shakers fashioned their own tacks, rivets, and nails to build with; they hand knit strips of fabric that would be woven into chair seats. While they separat-ed themselves from the outside world, they were still able to utilize technological advances made there. Such progress allowed the Shakers to live separately yet share state-of-the-art achievements with the rest of the world. Later, some communities even indulged in the purchase of cars, and other benefits of modernization, which they felt would make their way of life more attractive to potential converts.

While sharing these things with the World, the furniture, clothing, and buildings they created were outward symbols of the connectedness of their inner life and their work. Beauty was dictated by usefulness; if something was not necessary there was no reason to create it.

No new Shaker communities were established between 1840 and 1850, and within the next twenty years the population actually declined. Due to westward expansion, and changes brought about by the Civil War and rapid industrialization, the World—upon which the Shakers relied for converts— had changed enormously. Expansion of cities and the conveniences of increased technology and the availability of jobs in the World made communal living seemingly less and less attractive. As second-generation Shakers died and few new converts came in, communities gradually diminished. The Tyringham, Massachusetts, community was the first to close down completely, in 1875. By 1900 the entire Shaker legion consisted only of 2000 members. Today just one Shaker community remains, in Sabbathday Lake, Maine. However, their creations—now recognized by designers, architects, and laypeople in America and throughout the world for their immense quality and beauty—are very much in evidence in the revised Shaker villages and open-air museums, which endure as an acknowledgment of their optimism and strength.

above: An overhead view of the Hancock, Massachusetts, Shaker village.

opposite page: This three-story dairy barn is the only round Shaker barn, and an architectural milestone that captures the attention of visitors from across the nation. The barn is progressive in both its organization and its assembly. All three floors—each with a different purpose: for housing wagons, cattle, or manure—were accessible by ramps. The central haymow eased the farmer's work as it was only a few feet from the stalls. The barn was rebuilt in 1864 after a fire damaged it and numerous improvements were made, including the addition of clerestory windows and a central ventilator to decrease the chance of fire. The barn was fully restored in 1968.

Rocking chair

Originally created for use in Shaker communities, Shaker-built chairs were sold to the World as an added source of income from the late 1700s through the 1920s. New Lebanon was a main source of such trade, and chairs were the only furnishings used for this purpose. This rocking chair, as is typical with all Shaker furniture, is delicate and easy to move, yet solidly constructed to withstand years of use with minimal repairs. It is also a fine example of the use of naturally patterned wood to enhance the overall design.

Circa 1850
Probably New Lebanon, New York
Bird's-eye maple, replacement canvas-tape seat
45 x 21 1/4 x 22 1/2 in.
The Sherman Collection

Table

An example of the archetypal Hancock table, with its small brass pull and the beading on the bottom edge. Note that the drawer tapers to conform to the angle of the splayed legs.

Circa 1825–1850
Hancock, Massachusetts
Butternut, red stain, pine secondary, brass pull
26 x 30 5/8 x 20 5/8 in.
Collection of Mrs. C. B. Falls

Work Table

This detail of a small work table,
with its uniform warm color that the
Shakers liked, is quite revealing.
It is made from a mixture of woods,
mainly of black cherry with a
butternut rim to retain small objects.
The large lower drawer with its handle
on the left side is a later addition.
The leg shown is elegantly slender.

1825–1850
New Lebanon, New York
25 x 29 1/8 x 18 1/8 in.

Work table with hinged work surface and drawer

Circa 1845
Canterbury, New Hampshire
Private collection

Case of drawers

This beautifully detailed and carefully crafted case of drawers was originally built into the wall of a workshop, as was much Shaker furniture. The impeccable care and attention to detail so typical of the Shakers is evident in the construction of this piece. The drawers are arranged, top to bottom, from one to three inches in height, with no two drawers on one side being the same size. The case is constructed of 166 interior partitions which were notched for easy viewing. The original numbered labels have been discovered in several of the drawers, along with pencil inscriptions on their undersides.

Circa 1825–1850
New Lebanon, New York
Pine case, red orange stain, butternut drawer fronts, maple drawer partitions, apple or maple pulls
21 1/2 x 39 1/2 x 9 7/8 in.
The Shaker Museum, Old Chatham, New York

One side of the interior of the meetinghouse
at Canterbury, New Hampshire, shows the original
dark blue paint. All the interiors of the meetinghouses
were to be finished in this color. The two parallel blue
lines on either side of the window are Shaker pegboard
rails, which have always given Shaker buildings their
unique spare and functional look.

The Shakers of Kentucky
differed from their brothers
and sisters in the Northeast
by using arches and thus giving
a lighter and perhaps even more
elegant look to their buildings.
Again, the expensive dark blue
trim was used in their
important buildings and rooms.
This is a view into the
communal dining room
at Pleasant Hill.

Case of drawers

This case of drawers from a western community is much
more decorative than the standard Shaker design.
While the Shakers would never alter wood by painting
or varnishing it, the combination of three naturally
enhanced woods—the tiger maple, cherry, and
bird's eye maple—embellishes the drama of the piece.
The piece itself is rather simply but sturdily built;
this allowed for mobility, which was a concern since
communal furniture was moved from place to place.
A piece with the visual power of this is a product of the
more liberal western communities; being farther from
the Parent Ministry, western Shakers were apt to take
more freedom with their designs.

Circa 1850
Union Village, Ohio
Tiger-maple case, flaming-cherry drawer fronts,
pine, poplar, and walnut
53 7/8 x 46 1/4 x 23 7/8 in.
Collection Edwin Hibarger

Chest with drawers

The origins of this chest are unclear
as it possesses elements similar to
those both in the Enfield and the
Canterbury communities.

The panels and drawers resemble the style
of woodwork in the Ministry Shop in
Canterbury. However, a similar chest which
was also discovered at Canterbury has been
directly linked to Enfield. It is likely that
the chest was built in the Ministry Shop
by a Brother Joseph Johnson who divided
his time between the two communities.
Note the unusual panels on the lid.

Circa 1848
Enfield or Canterbury, New Hampshire
Pine, dark red orange paint, hardwood pulls,
iron hinges and lock, brass escutcheon
29 1/4 x 49 5/8 x 21 5/8 in.
Private collection

23

Long work table with turned legs
Circa 1835, New Lebanon, New York, Private collection

The washstand was a very important piece
in a Shaker dwelling. In accordance with the
Millenial Laws of 1821, cleanliness was among
the tenets of Shaker life; even wearing
"ragged clothes" to the workplace was
considered an offense against the Church.
Usually each sleeping room had its own
washstand, although in some dwellings
there was a common washroom
for each sex on each floor.

1862
James V. Calver
New Lebanon, New York
Pine, ocher stain, poplar drawer bottoms,
hardwood pulls
40 1/4 x 27 5/8 x 18 1/2 in.
Private collection

Looking down from the orchard at Sabbathday Lake, Maine, this view shows the herb garden and the meetinghouse. This Shaker village still actively grows and dries a variety of herbs, which are packaged in the community and distributed for sale to the World's people. At the left of center is the ministry shop, which now serves as a living history museum for visitors. The meetinghouse in this village is the only one still being used for worship.

Raised blanket chest with butter churn
and three baskets

This compact place specifically designed to
store blankets, eased the Shakers' clean-up
efforts and was durable and aesthetically
appealing as well. Like other furnishings,
the chest would be moved from place
to place over a span of time.

Circa 1830
Alfred, Maine
Blue paint on pine with lift-top
25 x 49 1/2 x 18 in.

Six-drawer work counter with sliding work surfaces
(with boxes and hog scraper candlestick)

The Shakers eschewed ornamentation in their
creations, yet the harmony of shape and
subtle detail make them visually attractive.
These objects are representative of the simple yet
attractive Shaker style. Believers preferred wooden
drawer pulls to the showier brass handles for their
drawers. The use of bright, solid colors prevailed
among the group to give visual appeal, particularly
to woodenware. The counter and boxes
were made from local wood.

Circa 1845
New Lebanon, New York
Private collection

Dwarf tall clock mechanism

A son of a clock-maker, Benjamin Youngs, Sr., was
himself a clock-maker in the village of Watervliet,
New York, where he moved his family in the 1790s.
Today there are at least twelve clocks built by
Youngs, Sr., still in existence. Clocks, and to an
even lesser extent watches, were not very common
in Shaker communities; bells were relied on most
often to awaken people and to announce meetings
and mealtimes. However, each family usually had
one clock. This clock, in fact, is an alarm clock on
which the center dial is turned to set the time.
Responsible for building the works of the clock,
Youngs, Sr., definitely had input into the creation
of the case as well; the simple yet elegant design,
the use of special woods, and the inscription on
the inside face of the clock show the influence
of his Shaker experiences.

1814
Benjamin Youngs, Sr. (1736–1818)
Watervliet, New York
Cherry case, pine back, glass, brass works
and pendulum, lead weights, iron hands and dial
(painted off-white on front and dark red on back)
54 x 10 x 7 in.
Art Complex Museum, Duxbury, Massachusetts

Shaker clock

Circa 1794
Canterbury, New Hampshire
Cherrywood
Signed John Winkley
37 x 9 x 4 in.

Cupboard
shown with wood bowl and baskets

Circa 1845
New Lebanon, New York
Red wash with pine gray interior
78 x 24 1/2 x 15 1/2
Private collection

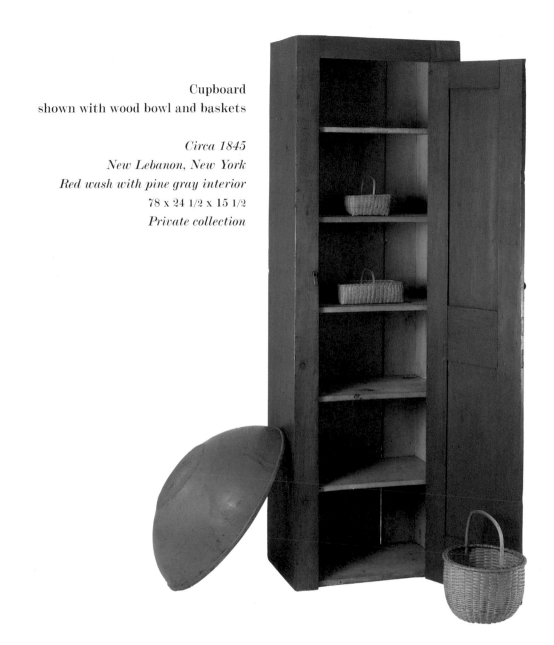

Chest on chest of drawers
with large oval box

Circa 1840–1860
Enfield, Connecticut

Meetinghouse benches

Shaker benches were made
in different lengths for ease
of movement and changes
of use in meetinghouses
and gathering rooms.
This slender furniture,
without stretchers between the
legs, is still firm and in use.
Shakers always moved their
benches and chairs around by
lifting the seat, not the back,
to avoid weakening the joints.

The interior of the Ministry Shop at Sabbathday Lake, Maine.
The wood-burning cast-iron stove provided heat, and the room
was kept immaculate by the Sisters' daily sweeping up of the
resulting ash. The built-in drawer case and the peg board
are also typical features of Shaker rooms.

Three oval carriers

Carriers are actually boxes with handles
added to allow for transport. They were
used, like the boxes, both in homes and
workplaces. Carriers came in a wide
variety of shapes and sizes. Usually
handles extended all the way to the
bottom of the box, as shown here.
There are only two or three existing
examples of carriers with movable
handles, made using copper tacks and
washers. Other carriers were specifically
designed for transporting sewing notions
and these were lined with satin or other
fabrics. The Shakers liked the effect
of the colored stains, which gave
the wood a finish, but allowed the grain
to show through.

Left: Circa 1840–1870
Probably Canterbury, New Hampshire
Maple, pine bottom, ash (?) handle,
yellow stain, copper tacks
8 x 12 7/8 x 9 3/8 in.
Private collection

Center: Circa 1860
Canterbury, New Hampshire
Maple, pine bottom, ash (?) handle,
red and ocher stain, copper tacks
7 x 10 7/8 x 7 3/4 in.
Private collection

Right: Circa 1840–1870
Probably Canterbury, New Hampshire
Maple, ash (?) bottom and handle,
yellow stain, copper tacks
7 x 9 x 6 5/8 in.
Private collection

Oval boxes

Like their chairs, Shaker oval boxes have become
an archetypal shape. Although they did not
organize the design, the manufacture and use in
many sizes by Shaker communities typified their
dictum for neatness and putting things away. The
boxes were used to store practically any small
solid objects; dry goods, or sewing notions.
Shaker historian June Sprigg has suggested that
this box could accommodate a sister's bonnet.
Sometimes a box was made to be presented by one
Shaker to another.

The boxes were produced in large quantities for
sale to the World's people. This fine example has
six swallowtail joins; there were usually five or
less. Note the alignment of the copper tacks.

Maple sides, 8 1/4 x 15 1/8 x 11 1/8

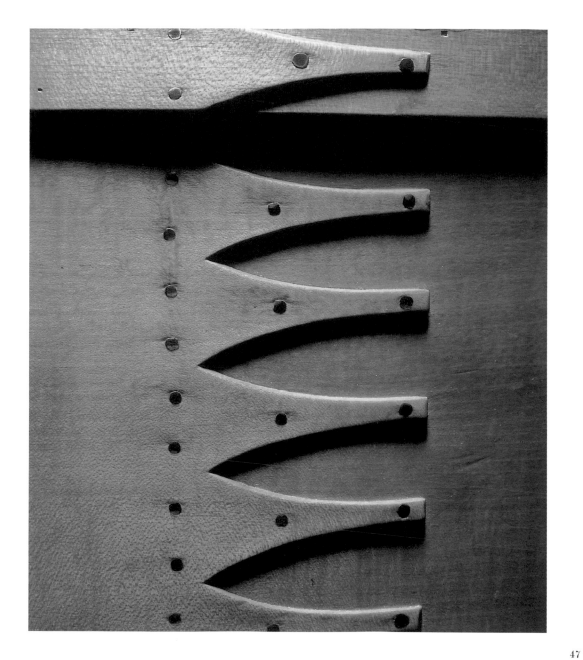

Oval box

Such boxes as this were emblematic of
Shaker design. The beautiful yet practical
containers were created in a wide variety of
shapes and sizes to suit almost any purpose.
The side joints, characteristic of Shaker work,
were an adaptation from the outside World.
They allowed for the swelling and shrinking of
the wood, which decreased the chance of damage.
Wooden boxes, aside from being purposeful,
were one of the few items Shakers were
permitted to own individually, and
they were often given as gifts.

Circa 1825–1850
Probably New Lebanon, New York
Maple, pine bottom and lid,
dark olive green paint, copper tacks
5 3/4 x 13 5/8 x 9 5/8 in.
Private collection

This detail shows the carving of the side joints,
or fingers, a distinctive feature of Shaker boxes.
The joints were cut with a knife to keep the edges
beveled and rounded, so as not to catch on anything
and break off. Copper tacks were used instead of iron,
as they do not rust or discolor.

Box

The Shakers normally built boxes, such as this one,
for storing bonnets while traveling. The pegs are an
adaptation from the World that the Shakers used
throughout their homes, meetinghouses, and workshops.
Originally designed to hang clothes—hence the original
name "clothes pins"—the Shakers later adapted many
items specifically to hang on pegs. Chairs, mirrors, tools,
and even clocks were built specifically to hang from these
pins, making use and clean up more efficient.

Circa 1850
Enfield, Connecticut
Maple, dark olive green paint, birch or maple pegs,
brass hinges and lock, iron latch
13 x 17 1/2 x 14 3/8 in.
Collection of Mr. and Mrs. Gustave G. Nelson

Shakers created baskets in a large variety of shapes and forms and for many different purposes—from holding sewing notions to carrying laundry to draining cheese curds. Depending on its purpose, the traditional shape was adapted and enhanced. For example, this large, two-handled basket was probably used to carry the heavy loads harvested from the fields. In typical Shaker style, details add both to the beauty and the usefulness of the object: the two handles allow two workers to transport the harvest from the fields. This basket, as are most Shaker baskets, is made from ash, which allows for flexibility in shaping and bending. Baskets were often inscribed with the owner's initials for identification.

Probably Alfred or Sabbathday, Maine
Black or brown ash, hardwood handles
14 1/2 x 22 in. diameter
The United Society of Shakers, Sabbathday Lake, Maine

These Shaker baskets are shown on two trestled
meetinghouse benches. The seats are made of pine and
the supports are chestnut.

The original shapes and patterns of Shaker baskets are
thought to have derived from the methods of the Northeast
Indians. Eventually the Shakers found them not durable
enough for continuous use. They increased the thickness of
the splints and with Shaker-designed wooden molds, stronger,
more uniform baskets were manufactured for the communities
and for the World's people.

This wonderful combination of cupboard
and drawers from Mount Lebanon, New York,
was evidently carefully planned, thus provoking
our late twentieth-century minds to ponder
what early nineteenth-century office activity
was contained within these variously
sized drawers and doors.

Patent model for side chair with tilts

The tilts on this chair were invented as a way
to reduce wear and tear on floors and carpets.
Although this was originally thought to be a
good innovation, the hollowing out of the leg
bottoms and the drilling did weaken the chair
at the point of greatest stress.
George O. Donnell originated the idea
of making tilts in metal and
attaching them to the rear legs.

It was indeed unusual for Shakers to seek
patents, although they innovated numerous
design and building elements, so this is an
especially unusual piece.

The woven chair-seat tape is a feature
common to Shaker furniture. Most tapes were
colorful and patterned. In the early 1800s the
tapes were hand-knit, but later it was found
more efficient to buy cotton tapes.

1852
George O. Donnell
New Lebanon, New York
Bird's-eye maple, brass tilts, replacement red,
white, and blue woven woolen seat.
15 1/2 x 11 x 8 3/4 in.
Collection of David A. Schorsch

Five side chairs

Circa 1840
Canterbury or Enfield, New Hampshire
Private collection

Rocking chair with scrolled arms

Circa 1830
New Lebanon, New York
Private collection

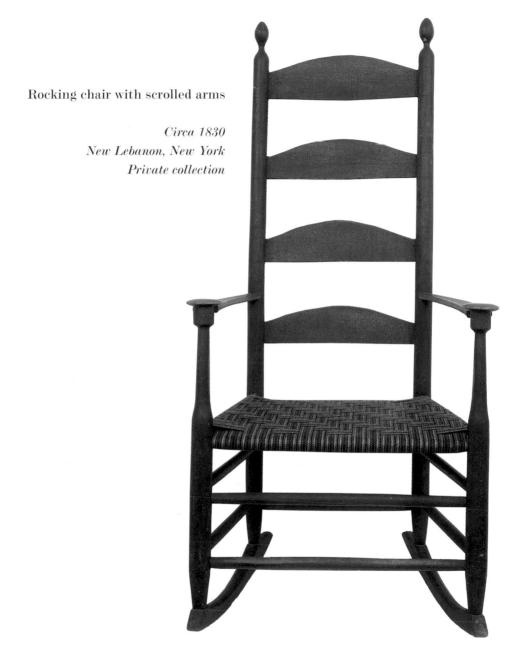

Cast-iron woodstove

This stove has a superheater and
a built-in hanger for shovel and tongs.

Circa 1840
Probably New Lebanon, New York
Collection of Hancock Shaker Village,
Pittsfield, Massachusetts

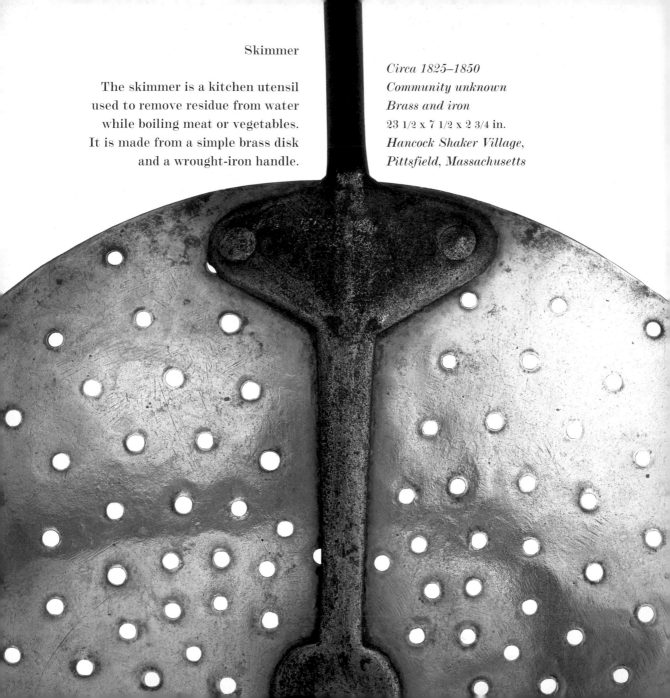

Skimmer

The skimmer is a kitchen utensil
used to remove residue from water
while boiling meat or vegetables.
It is made from a simple brass disk
and a wrought-iron handle.

Circa 1825–1850
Community unknown
Brass and iron
23 1/2 x 7 1/2 x 2 3/4 in.
Hancock Shaker Village,
Pittsfield, Massachusetts

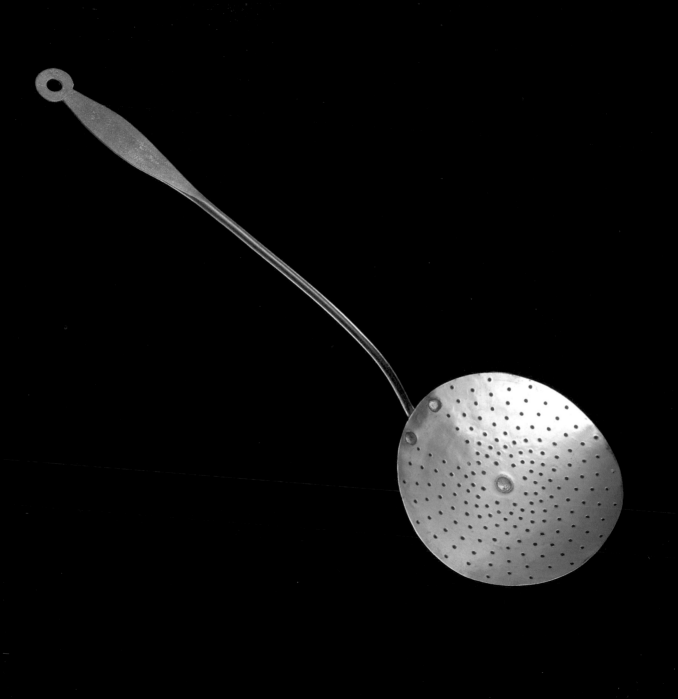

Knit Carpet

This very colorful knit carpet is emblematic of a time when the Shakers lessened the restrictions they placed on themselves and the items they created. Previously this carpet would have been shunned as too ornamental but, in the late 1800s, the Shakers were allowing themselves such pleasures as wall paper, painted china, and framed pictures. The bright colors and lively patterns were accomplished through the technique of plying, in which at least two colors are knitted together in each section. Each row is a separate section of knitting attached to the others, beginning with the center ring, which has been knitted into the form of a tube, then flattened and stitched into a spiral. This is an example of highly skilled knitting.

Circa 1890–1895
Probably Hancock, Massachusetts
Red, blue, yellow, brown, white, and orange wool yarn, and red, white, and blue braided cloth border.
49 in. (diameter)
Collection of George W. Sieber

In the larger Shaker buildings, most of the shelving was built into the walls. And with the higher ceilings like those preferred in Kentucky, movable steps were needed to put everything in its place.

Set of steps

Circa 1830–1850
Pine
30 x 18 1/2 x 23
Enfield, Connecticut
Private collection

preceding pages

An afternoon in a room of the Church Family
Dwelling in Hancock, Massachusetts.
The wall clock is one of a group of six made
by a Shaker Brother from the adjoining
community of New Lebanon, New York.
There is no inscription on the face of the clock,
because Brother Youngs preferred just to add
his signature on the back.
The deep side-paneled windows have wooden
thumb screws which allowed the lower window
to slide up to a chosen level.

Case of drawers on base with drawer

Circa 1830
Attributed to Thomas Hammond, Jr.
Harvard, Massachusetts
Collection of Hancock Shaker Village,
Pittsfield, Massachusetts

Small cupboard and case of drawers

The single drawer pulls were popular for the efficiency they allowed: single pulls, as opposed to double pulls, made opening the drawer much easier. Single pulls were used for both built-in and free-standing drawer cases.

Circa 1830
Probably New Lebanon, New York
Collection of Hancock Shaker Village,
Pittsfield, Massachusetts

Tripod stand (with table swift)

The tripod stands are wonderful examples of
the Shaker combination of grace and
usefulness. While elegant and sophisticated
looking, these stands were easily moved
and stored, a necessity in the communities.

Circa 1825
New Lebanon, New York
Private collection

Tilt-top tripod stand

Circa 1840
Harvard, Massachusetts
Private collection

Tilt-top tripod stand

Circa 1840, Harvard, Massachusetts
Private collection

Three single-door cupboards

The two blue cupboards have raised panel doors with beaded trim, and angled feet.

Circa 1820
Original blue paint on pine
84 x 23 3/4 x 8
New Lebanon, New York

The red single door cupboard is from Harvard, Massachusetts.

Circa 1840
Pine, brass latch
58 x 19 x 8

Baskets

Baskets are perhaps most emblematic of the
Shaker aesthetic: they were essential and
functional, and therefore could be made to look
quite beautiful. Baskets were for use by the
community as well as for sale outside. They were
most often made from oak, ash, or willow splint
and came in a wide variety of shapes and sizes
and for numerous purposes.

Circa 1835–1870
New Lebanon, New York
Collection of Hancock Shaker Village,
Pittsfield, Massachusetts

This small desk under the window of the Fruitlands Museum, in Harvard, Massachusetts, is from the Shaker community that was established nearby. The desk shows sewing implements that Shaker Sisters in many communities used to make "fancy goods" for sale to the World's people.

Centre Family Dwelling

This four-story limestone building
took ten years to complete and is a
landmark in Shaker architecture.
The dwelling is forty-six feet high
and sixty feet wide; each of the
second-floor windows is seven feet
high and the front doors—one side for
the Brothers' entry, the other for the
Sisters'—are ten feet tall from top to
bottom. The building consisted of
a large dining hall, a smaller dining
room for the Ministry members,
a meetingroom, sleeping quarters,
a kitchen and food storage area in
the cellar, and an attic for clothing
storage. This stately and refined
building captivated fellow Shakers as
well as visitors from the outside world.

1824–1834
Pleasant Hill, Kentucky

Automobile garage

This garage was built in 1908, the year after the Shakers
at Canterbury, eager to include modern technology in
their lives, purchased their first car. The garage housed
the car with the tower serving as a storage place
for the hoses used for the community's fire engine.
By utilizing pressed metal siding the Shakers
updated the overall look of the community
in an attempt to interest more converts.

Canterbury, New Hampshire
1908

Ministry Workshop

This side view of a building at Pleasant Hill is illustrative of the basic yet elegant Shaker architecture. This building follows the Millenial Law of 1845 which prohibited the use of unnecessary embellishments in their architecture. The Law even dictated the proper color of paint for specific buildings—light for wooden buildings, red or blue for barns and houses, and white for meetinghouses only.

1820
Pleasant Hill, Kentucky

The Tree of Life

The most popular Shaker inspirational drawing. This image is borrowed
freely today, by antique dealers for their business cards, gift shops for
design themes and country restaurants for their menu covers.
The Tree of Life is quite different from other Shaker gift drawings,
which are typically full of emblems and compartmentalized sayings
finished in fine penwork and delicate coloring.
This was painted and colored boldly with curved branches
that change the first impression of ordered symmetry.

Hannah Cohoon
1788–1864
18 1/8 x 23 1/4
Hancock, Massachusetts

Plan of Canterbury, New Hampshire

This map is one of the largest and most detailed plans that
survives. Although decorative paintings were shunned in
Shaker communities, such plans were allowed, both as an aid
to future building and as a sort of spiritual document recording
the Shakers' existence as a religious sect. While rendering the
plan of Canterbury with great detail and care, it is obvious
by the use of color and flourishes to the lettering,
that the artist took joy in creating it.

1848
Henry Clay Blinn
Canterbury, New Hampshire
Brown, blue, and black ink and watercolor on off-white paper
38 x 80 3/4 in.
Shaker Village, Inc., Canterbury, New Hampshire

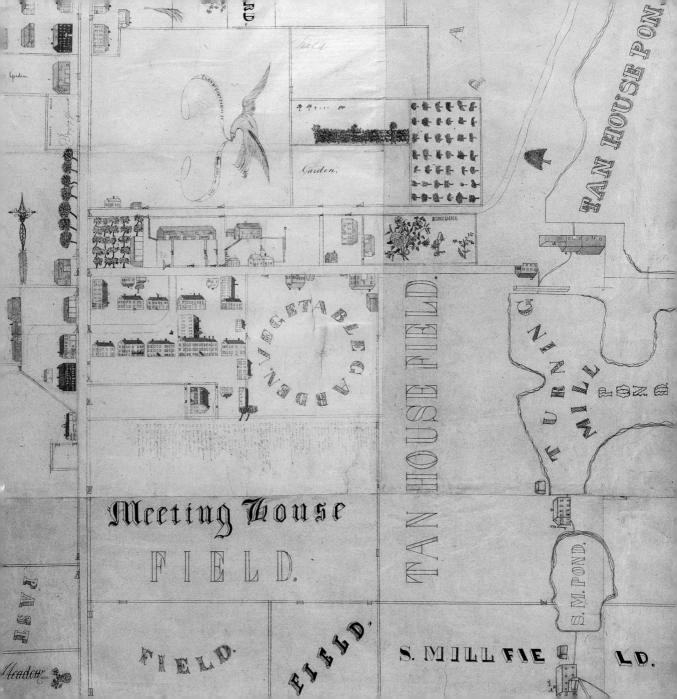

TAN HOUSE POND

Garden.

BOTANIC GARDEN.

TURNING MILL POND

TAN HOUSE FIELD.

VEGETABLE GARDEN.

S. M. POND.

Meeting House

FIELD.

FIELD.

FIELD.

S. MILL FIE LD.

PAST

Meadow

Many of the buildings and much of the furniture shown in this book
can be seen at the following sites:

Hancock Shaker Village, Pittsfield, Massachusetts.

Shakertown at Pleasant Hill, Harrodsburg, Kentucky.

Shaker Village, Inc., and the Canterbury Shakers, Canterbury, New Hampshire.

Fruitlands Museums, Harvard, Massachusetts.

United Society of Shakers, Sabbathday Lake, Maine.

Shakertown, South Union, Kentucky.

The Shaker Museum, Old Chatham, New York.

Darrow School/Mount Lebanon Shaker Village, New Lebanon, New York.

Old Sturbridge Village, Sturbridge, Massachusetts.

Town of Harvard, Massachusetts.

Town of Colonie, New York.